W9-BUB-028

U.S.A. TRAVEL GUIDES

MINNESOTA

BY ANN HEINRICHS • ILLUSTRATED BY MATT KANIA

The Child's World®
childsworld.com

Published by The Child's World®
1980 Lookout Drive • Mankato, MN 56003-1705
800-599-READ • www.childsworld.com

Photo Credits

Photographs ©: Andrey Krav/iStockphoto, cover, 1; Marie Pearson, 7; U.S. Fish and Wildlife Service, 8; International Falls Area Chamber of Commerce, 11; National Park Service, 12, 15; Shutterstock Images, 16, 37 (top), 37 (bottom); Andre Jenny Stock Connection Worldwide/Newscom, 19; Steve Kohls/Brainerd Daily Dispatch/AP Images, 20; Walter Bibikow/Mauritius/SuperStock, 23; Chad Kainz CC2.0, 24; Andre Jenny Stock Connection Worldwide/Newscom, 27; Carol M. Highsmith/Carol M. Highsmith Archive/Library of Congress, 28, 31; Tommy Liggett/Shutterstock Images, 32; thalling55 CC2.0, 35

ISBN 9781503819634
LCCN 2016961176

Printing

Printed in the United States of America
PA02334

Ann Heinrichs is the author of more than 100 books for children and young adults. She has also enjoyed successful careers as a children's book editor and an advertising copywriter. Ann grew up in Fort Smith, Arkansas, and lives in Chicago, Illinois.

post card

About the Author
Ann Heinrichs

Matt Kania loves maps and, as a kid, dreamed of making them. In school he studied geography and cartography, and today he makes maps for a living. Matt's favorite thing about drawing maps is learning about the places they represent. Many of the maps he has created can be found in books, magazines, videos, Web sites, and public places.

post card

About the
Map Illustrator
Matt Kania

On the cover: Minneapolis has lots of places to visit!

OUR MINNESOTA TRIP

MINNESOTA

Ready for a grand tour of Minnesota? You'll be glad you came! It's chock-full of things to discover.

You'll watch people carve canoes. You'll hear moose grunt and wolves howl. You'll run your hands through animal furs. You'll pick vegetables and churn butter. You'll learn where Native American peace pipes come from. You'll see people bowl with frozen turkeys. And you'll walk right across the Mississippi River!

There's much more to explore, so buckle up. You can follow that loopy dotted line. Or else just skip around. Minnesota, here we come!

As you travel through Minnesota, watch for all the interesting facts along the way.

WELCOME TO MINNESOTA

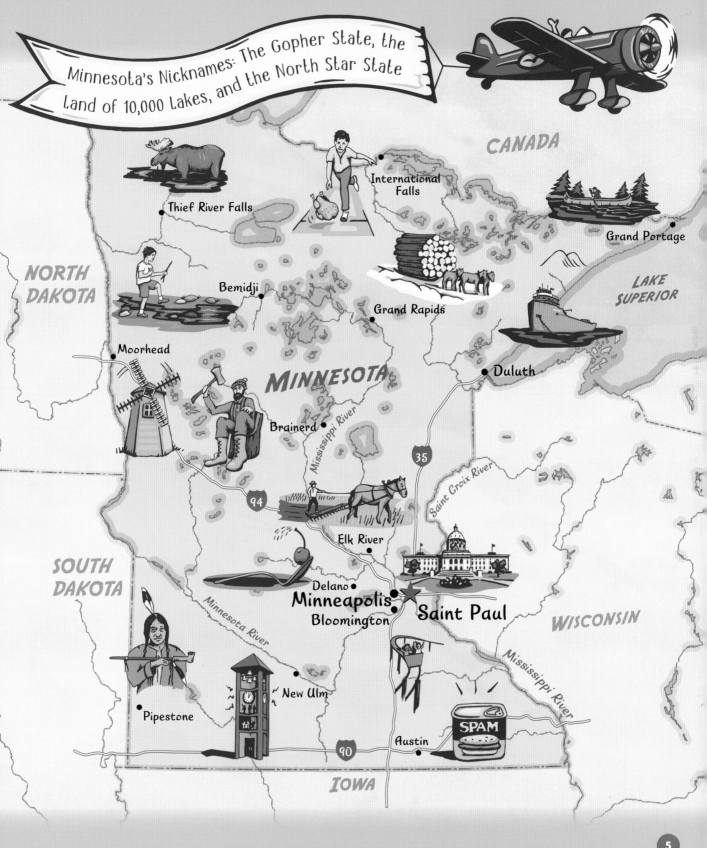

Minnesota's Nicknames: The Gopher State, the Land of 10,000 Lakes, and the North Star State

CANADA

Thief River Falls

International Falls

Grand Portage

NORTH DAKOTA

Bemidji

Grand Rapids

LAKE SUPERIOR

Moorhead

MINNESOTA

Duluth

Brainerd

Mississippi River

35

Saint Croix River

94

Elk River

SOUTH DAKOTA

Minnesota River

Delano

Minneapolis

Bloomington

Saint Paul

WISCONSIN

Mississippi River

Pipestone

New Ulm

Austin

90

SPAM

IOWA

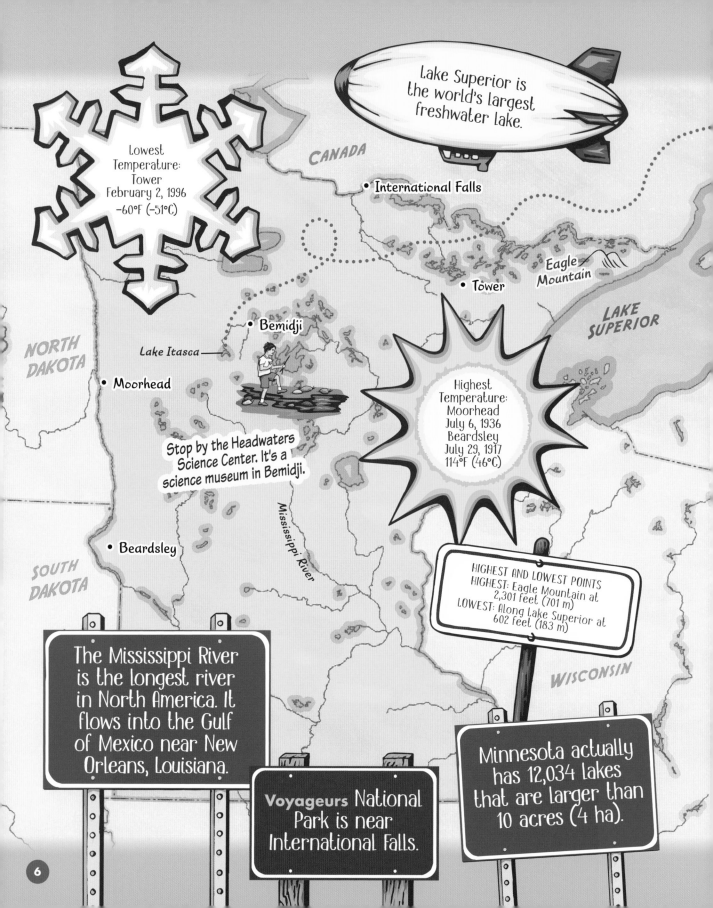

Lake Superior is the world's largest freshwater lake.

CANADA

• International Falls

Eagle Mountain

• Tower

LAKE SUPERIOR

Lowest Temperature:
Tower
February 2, 1996
–60°F (–51°C)

• Bemidji

Lake Itasca

NORTH DAKOTA

• Moorhead

Stop by the Headwaters Science Center. It's a science museum in Bemidji.

Highest Temperature:
Moorhead
July 6, 1936
Beardsley
July 29, 1917
114°F (46°C)

• Beardsley

SOUTH DAKOTA

Mississippi River

HIGHEST AND LOWEST POINTS
HIGHEST: Eagle Mountain at 2,301 feet (701 m)
LOWEST: Along Lake Superior at 602 feet (183 m)

WISCONSIN

The Mississippi River is the longest river in North America. It flows into the Gulf of Mexico near New Orleans, Louisiana.

Voyageurs National Park is near International Falls.

Minnesota actually has 12,034 lakes that are larger than 10 acres (4 ha).

WHERE THE MISSISSIPPI RIVER BEGINS

Want to cross the Mississippi River? You can do it on foot! Just go to Lake Itasca, near Bemidji. It's the source of the Mississippi River. You can wade across the river where it begins. Or leap across on stepping-stones. Just watch out! Those rocks are slippery!

Minnesota is called the Land of 10,000 Lakes. Lake Itasca is just one of them. Lake Superior borders northeastern Minnesota. It's one of the nation's five Great Lakes.

Northern Minnesota is rough and rugged. The state's highest points are in this region. The rest of Minnesota is mostly rolling plains. They make rich farmland.

Stepping-stones mark the spot where Lake Itasca feeds the Mississippi River.

AGASSIZ NATIONAL WILDLIFE REFUGE

Do you hear a deep grunt or whine? It could be a moose! Do you hear howling? It could be a coyote or a wolf! Do you hear a crazy yodeling call? It could be a waterbird called a loon!

You're roaming through Agassiz National Wildlife Refuge. It's in northwestern Minnesota, near Thief River Falls.

Minnesota's forests are full of wildlife. You'll see big deer and little foxes. You'll glimpse sleek minks and otters. Fat woodchucks and muskrats waddle along. And giant Canada geese drift across the lakes. Just creep quietly and perk up your ears!

Agassiz Refuge's moose population may be declining because of disease, parasites, and warmer temperatures.

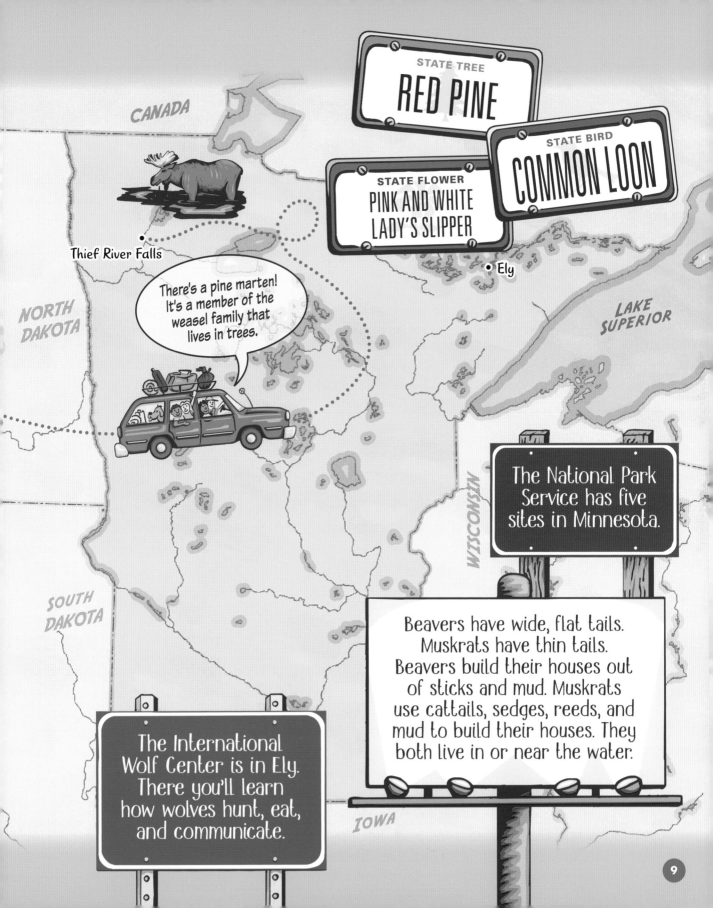

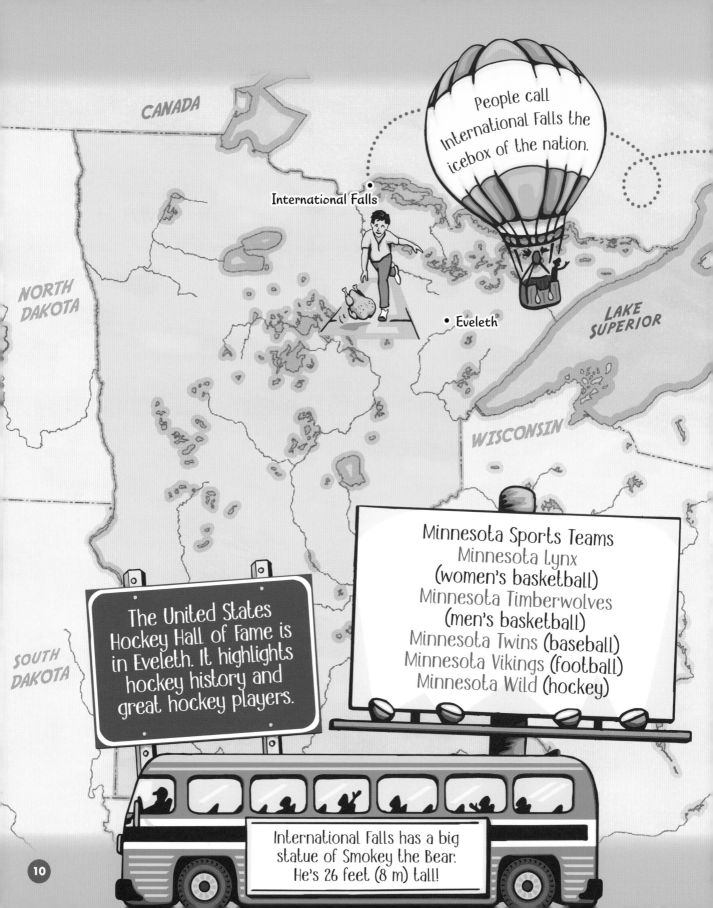

CANADA

People call International Falls the icebox of the nation.

International Falls

• Eveleth

LAKE SUPERIOR

NORTH DAKOTA

WISCONSIN

SOUTH DAKOTA

The United States Hockey Hall of Fame is in Eveleth. It highlights hockey history and great hockey players.

Minnesota Sports Teams
Minnesota Lynx (women's basketball)
Minnesota Timberwolves (men's basketball)
Minnesota Twins (baseball)
Minnesota Vikings (football)
Minnesota Wild (hockey)

International Falls has a big statue of Smokey the Bear. He's 26 feet (8 m) tall!

Let's enter the snowshoe race or the Freeze Yer Gizzard Blizzard Run!

ICEBOX DAYS IN INTERNATIONAL FALLS

Do you like winter sports? Then you'll love Icebox Days. It's a crazy festival of winter sports. You can try "smoosh" racing through the snow. Big boards are strapped to your feet. Or you might like turkey bowling. You'll use frozen turkeys instead of bowling balls!

Minnesota's a great place for winter fun. People enjoy skiing, sledding, snowmobiling, and ice-skating. Hockey is a popular team sport, too.

In warm weather, people head for the lakes. They go swimming, waterskiing, and fishing. The forests are great for hiking and camping. You'll enjoy Minnesota any time of the year!

Smoosh racing was invented near International Falls.

PIPESTONE NATIONAL MONUMENT

Feel the rough, red pipestone. It's soft and easy to carve. You're visiting Pipestone National Monument. It's in the town of Pipestone. You can watch a carving demonstration here. You'll learn how to carve and drill the stone.

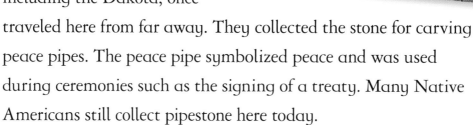

Native Americans, including the Dakota, once traveled here from far away. They collected the stone for carving peace pipes. The peace pipe symbolized peace and was used during ceremonies such as the signing of a treaty. Many Native Americans still collect pipestone here today.

Thousands of Dakotas once lived in Minnesota. They built rounded homes with branches and hides. They hunted forest animals for food. The Ojibwe, or Chippewa, arrived in the late 1600s. They came from Wisconsin, to the east.

You'll see lots of quartzite rock along the Circle Trail at Pipestone National Monument. The pipestone lies under the quartzite.

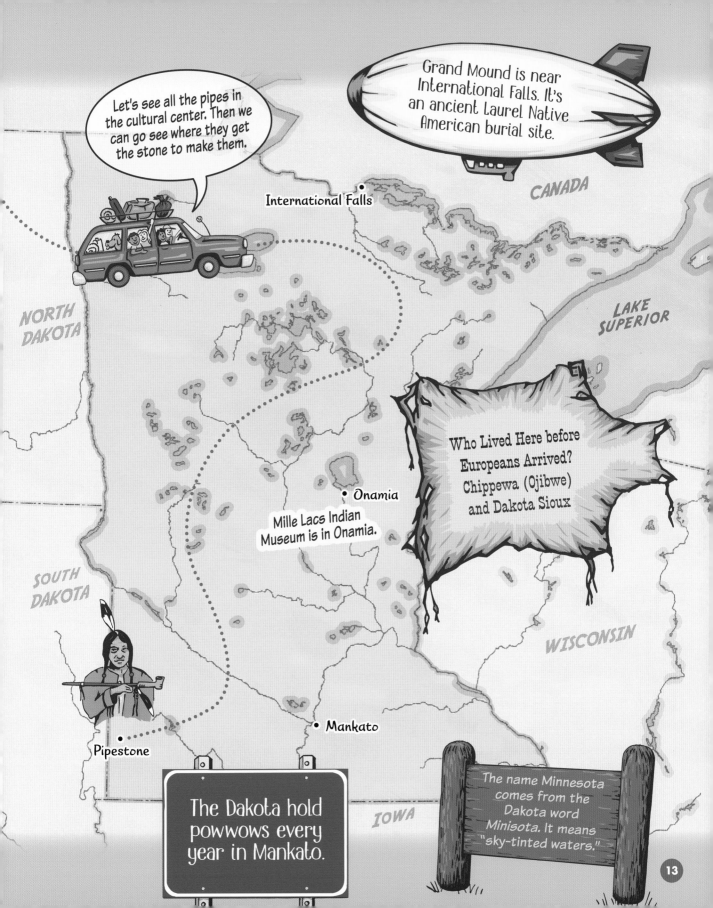

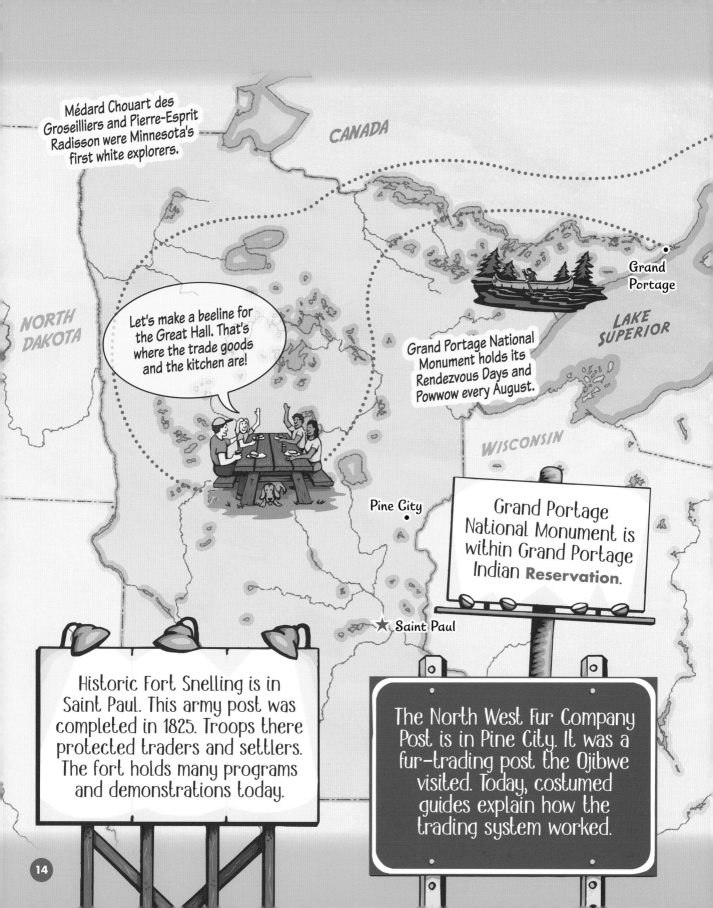

Médard Chouart des Groseilliers and Pierre-Esprit Radisson were Minnesota's first white explorers.

CANADA

Grand Portage

LAKE SUPERIOR

NORTH DAKOTA

Let's make a beeline for the Great Hall. That's where the trade goods and the kitchen are!

Grand Portage National Monument holds its Rendezvous Days and Powwow every August.

WISCONSIN

Pine City

Grand Portage National Monument is within Grand Portage Indian **Reservation**.

★ Saint Paul

Historic Fort Snelling is in Saint Paul. This army post was completed in 1825. Troops there protected traders and settlers. The fort holds many programs and demonstrations today.

The North West Fur Company Post is in Pine City. It was a fur-trading post the Ojibwe visited. Today, costumed guides explain how the trading system worked.

FUR TRADING AT GRAND PORTAGE

Run your hands through thick animal furs. Smell the freshly baked bread. See the canoes built by hand. You're visiting Grand Portage National Monument! It brings Minnesota's fur-trading days to life.

French fur traders arrived in about 1660. They were the first white people in Minnesota. Several fur companies soon moved in. They hired French-Canadian voyageurs. The voyageurs traveled by canoe and on foot. They went between trading posts and the wilderness.

Grand Portage was an important trading post. Voyageurs and the Ojibwe met and traded there. Every summer, they all gathered for a **rendezvous**. They exchanged goods, food, stories, and games.

Stop by the tinsmith during Rendezvous Days. You'll learn how to make a candleholder!

ELK RIVER'S OLIVER KELLEY FARM

Animals roam inside the barn. Farmworkers plow fields using oxen and horses. Fresh vegetables are growing in the garden. You're visiting the Oliver Kelley Farm!

This is a living history farm. It shows how farmers lived in the 1800s. The farmworkers all wear 1860s clothing. And they explain what they're doing.

Farming has always been important in Minnesota. Today, farms cover more than half the state. Hogs are the most common farm animals. Beef and dairy cattle are important, too. Corn and soybeans are the leading crops. They make great meals for farm animals!

Horses plow fields and power a grain-threshing machine at the Oliver Kelley Farm.

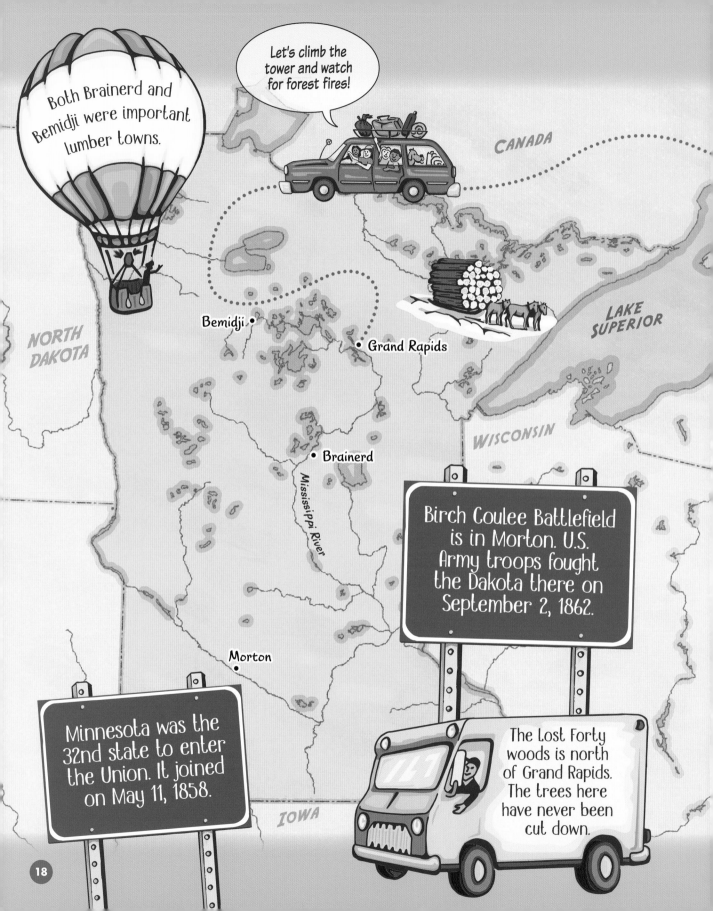

GRAND RAPIDS' FOREST HISTORY CENTER

Chat with the **lumberjacks**. They'll show you how they chop and saw. Next, climb aboard the wanigan. This shack floats on the Mississippi River. You're touring an old-time logging camp! It's at the Forest History Center in Grand Rapids.

Minnesota's logging **industry** began in the 1830s. Lumberjacks cut down millions of pine trees. At first, oxen pulled the logs by chains. Later, horses pulled the logs on sleighs.

The logs were floated down a river. Workers called river pigs rode atop the logs. They guided the logs along to sawmills. The logs were then sawed into lumber. The lumber was used to build homes, schools, and barns.

Logs float on the Mississippi River at the Forest History Center's logging camp.

PAUL BUNYAN, THE GIANT LUMBERJACK

The big guy winks his eyes and talks. So maybe he's not so scary after all. But he's taller than a two-story building!

He's Paul Bunyan. You'll find him at Paul Bunyan Land. It's at This Old Farm in Brainerd. But what's this giant all about?

Lumberjacks had an imaginary hero. He was a giant lumberjack named Paul Bunyan. His sidekick was Babe the Blue Ox. Lumberjacks used to tell **tall tales** about their hero.

Giant Paul Bunyan statues stand in many cities today. You'll find them in places where lumberjacks lived!

Minnesota is filled with tall tales about the legendary Paul Bunyan. One says he used giant mosquitoes to drill holes in trees.

Paul Bunyan will greet you by name if you stop by for a visit!

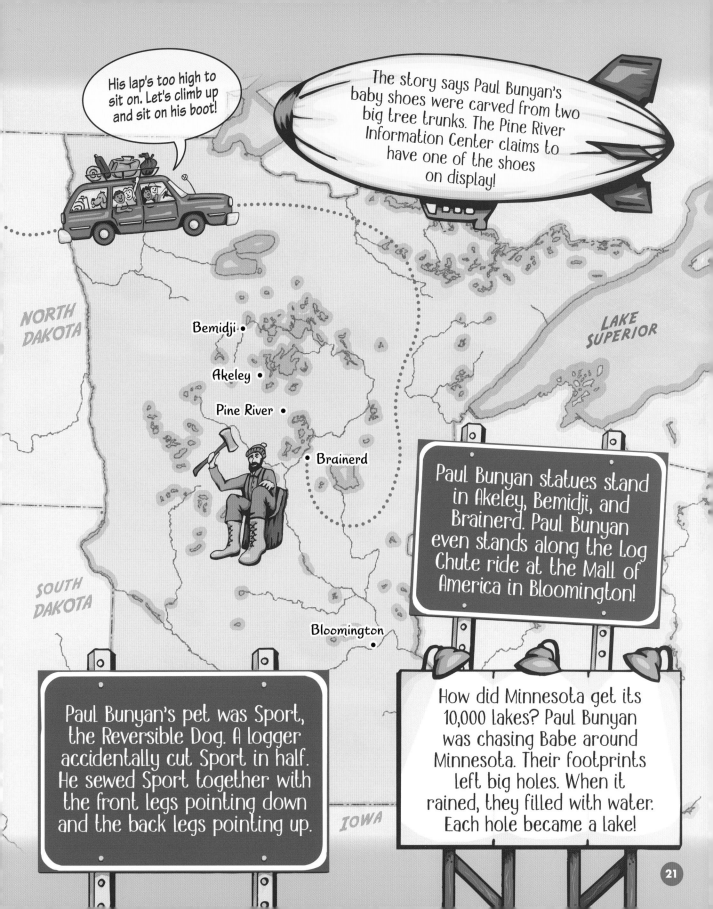

His lap's too high to sit on. Let's climb up and sit on his boot!

The story says Paul Bunyan's baby shoes were carved from two big tree trunks. The Pine River Information Center claims to have one of the shoes on display!

NORTH DAKOTA

LAKE SUPERIOR

Bemidji •

Akeley •

Pine River •

• Brainerd

SOUTH DAKOTA

Bloomington •

Paul Bunyan statues stand in Akeley, Bemidji, and Brainerd. Paul Bunyan even stands along the Log Chute ride at the Mall of America in Bloomington!

Paul Bunyan's pet was Sport, the Reversible Dog. A logger accidentally cut Sport in half. He sewed Sport together with the front legs pointing down and the back legs pointing up.

IOWA

How did Minnesota get its 10,000 lakes? Paul Bunyan was chasing Babe around Minnesota. Their footprints left big holes. When it rained, they filled with water. Each hole became a lake!

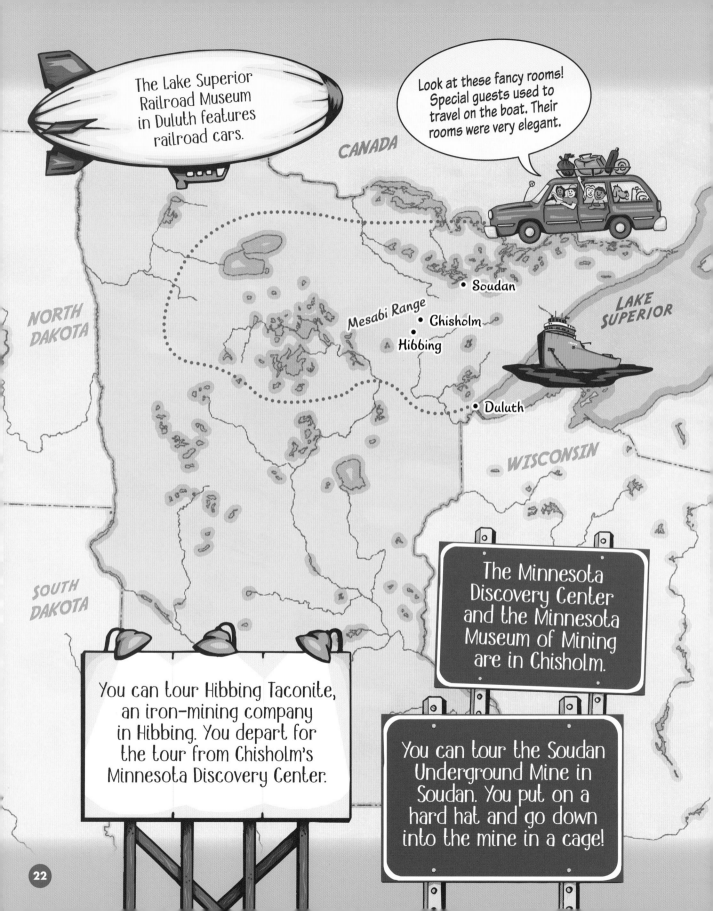

THE *WILLIAM A. IRVIN* IRON ORE BOAT

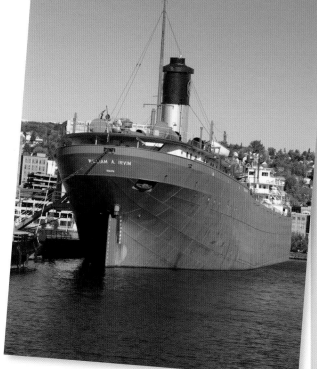

If you're in Duluth, head for the waterfront. There you'll climb aboard the *William A. Irvin*. It once carried iron **ore**. It sailed to ports along the Great Lakes. Sometimes it sailed through terrible storms.

The **cargo** area could hold thousands of tons of ore. Visit the engine rooms. The engines gave the boat 2,000 **horsepower**. That's about ten times more horsepower than an average car has!

Iron ore was first shipped from Minnesota in 1884. Minnesota soon became the leading iron-producing state. Thousands of **immigrants** came to northeastern Minnesota. The area's Mesabi Range was great for mining. It held massive deposits of iron ore.

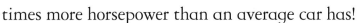

The William A. Irvin *carried both iron ore and rich guests during its more than 40 years of service.*

MOORHEAD'S HJEMKOMST FESTIVAL

See dancers in colorful folk costumes. See some spooky trolls. Try some *aebleskiver*. They're Danish pancake balls. Then have some *krumkake*, a Swedish and Norwegian cookie. Finish up with some delicious *vinatarta*. That's a layered Icelandic cake.

You're enjoying the Hjemkomst Festival! It celebrates Scandinavian **culture**. Scandinavians have roots in a group of countries. They are Norway, Sweden, Denmark, Finland, and Iceland.

Thousands of Scandinavians settled in Minnesota. Many were immigrants in the late 1800s. Their culture spread throughout the state. Scandinavians have a lot to celebrate!

The Hopperstad Stave Church at the Hjemkomst Center was carved out of pine, cedar, and redwood.

Saint Paul's Festival of Nations features the heritage of almost 100 ethnic groups!

Scandinavian explorer Leif Eriksson got to North America around the year 1000.

CANADA

NORTH DAKOTA

Fargo •• Moorhead

Moorhead celebrates the Hjemkomst Festival with the city of Fargo, North Dakota. It's just across the border.

WISCONSIN

POPULATION OF LARGEST CITIES
Minneapolis..................410,939
Saint Paul....................300,851
Rochester.................... 112,225

In 2016, 5,519,952 people lived in Minnesota. It's the 22nd-largest state by population.

Minneapolis • ★
Saint Paul

SOUTH DAKOTA

Rochester •

The Hjemkomst Center is in Moorhead. It's a museum of Scandinavian culture. Hjemkomst means "homecoming" in Norwegian.

IOWA

NEW ULM'S GLOCKENSPIEL

Clang, clang, clang! It's time for the Glockenspiel to play! That's the chiming clock tower in New Ulm. When it chimes, moving figures come out. They dance in a circle beneath the clock.

New Ulm is a very German town. German immigrants settled there in 1854.

Today, New Ulm still keeps many German **traditions**. Its festivals include Fasching and Oktoberfest. These festivals feature German music and food. People at Oktoberfest can even enjoy horse-drawn trolley rides through town.

There are 37 bells in the Glockenspiel. Together they weigh 2 tons (1.8 metric tons).

THE STATE CAPITOL IN SAINT PAUL

Minnesota's capitol is gleaming white. But something gold flashes out above the entrance. It's a huge sculpture called the Quadriga. It shows four golden horses pulling a golden carriage. You can get right up close to them, too. Just take a capitol tour!

The capitol houses many important state government offices. For example, the state legislature meets there. It's one of Minnesota's three branches of government. Its members make the state's laws. Another branch of government carries out the laws. This branch is led by the governor. The third branch consists of judges. They decide whether laws have been broken.

The Quadriga sits at the base of the dome at the front of the Minnesota capitol building.

Wow! I can see sunlight bouncing off those horses from blocks away!

Warren Burger was chief justice of the U.S. Supreme Court (1969-1986). He was born in Saint Paul.

CANADA

LAKE SUPERIOR

Minnesotans celebrated the capitol's centennial, or 100th birthday, in 2005.

NORTH DAKOTA

The Quadriga's horses represent the power of nature—earth, wind, fire, and water.

Minnesota's state motto is "L'étoile du nord." This is French for "The star of the North."

Maine •

SOUTH DAKOTA

Walter Mondale was vice president under President Jimmy Carter (1977-1981). He was born in Ceylon.

William O. Douglas was the longest-serving justice on the U.S. Supreme Court (1939-1975). He was born in Maine, Minnesota.

★ Saint Paul

Hubert Humphrey was vice president under President Lyndon B. Johnson (1965-1969). He was born in South Dakota but lived in Minnesota as an adult.

Ceylon
•

IOWA

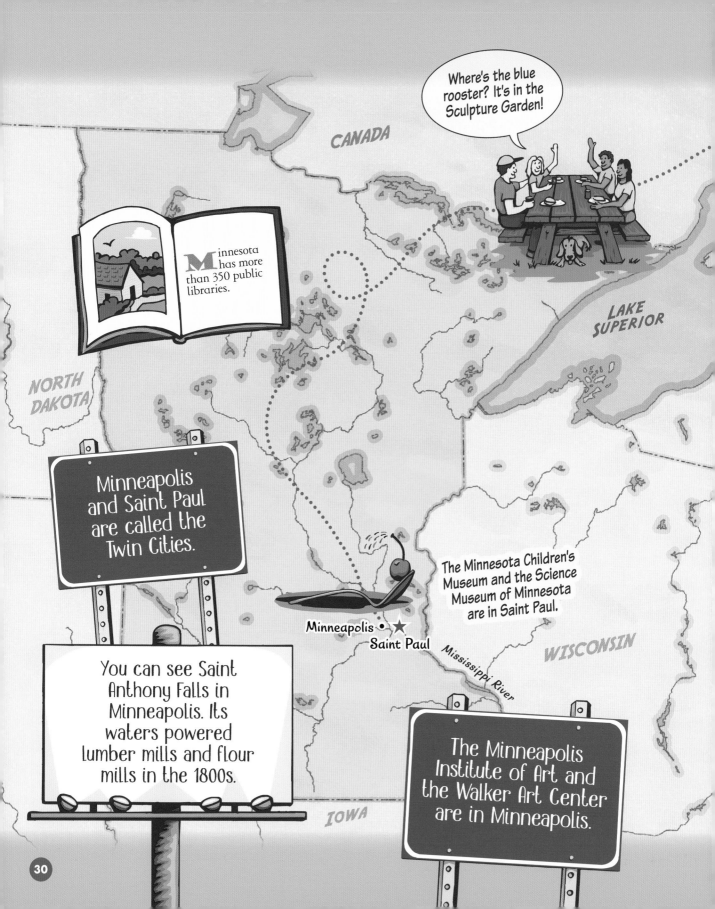

Where's the blue rooster? It's in the Sculpture Garden!

CANADA

Minnesota has more than 350 public libraries.

LAKE SUPERIOR

NORTH DAKOTA

Minneapolis and Saint Paul are called the Twin Cities.

The Minnesota Children's Museum and the Science Museum of Minnesota are in Saint Paul.

Minneapolis •
★
Saint Paul

Mississippi River

WISCONSIN

You can see Saint Anthony Falls in Minneapolis. Its waters powered lumber mills and flour mills in the 1800s.

The Minneapolis Institute of Art and the Walker Art Center are in Minneapolis.

IOWA

MINNEAPOLIS'S CHERRY AND SPOON

Do you like cherries? How about a cherry bigger than you? You'll see one in Minneapolis's Sculpture Garden. It's a giant cherry in a giant spoon. And the cherry's stem mists water!

There are many amazing sights in Minneapolis. Just take a walk along the riverfront. You'll see the huge Stone Arch Bridge. Then hop aboard a riverboat. You'll view the city from the Mississippi River. If you like shopping, stroll along Nicollet Mall. It's 12 blocks long!

To relax, head for one of Minneapolis's parks. You can ride a bike for miles. Or just lounge by a lake. There's something for everyone in Minneapolis!

Spoonbridge and Cherry *is an iconic sculpture in Minnesota.*

Do you like hanging out at the mall? Then check out the Mall of America. It's in Bloomington. It's the nation's largest mall under one roof!

This mall has more than 520 stores. But that's not all. It has a theme park called Nickelodeon Universe. It also has an aquarium with sharks. People come here from all over the world!

In the 1900s, Minnesota changed in many ways. Its service industries grew fast. Those are businesses that offer services, not goods. They include stores such as those in the mall. Many banks and hospitals opened, too. Rochester's Mayo Clinic became world-famous.

You'll find impressive LEGO sculptures at the LEGO Store in the Mall of America.

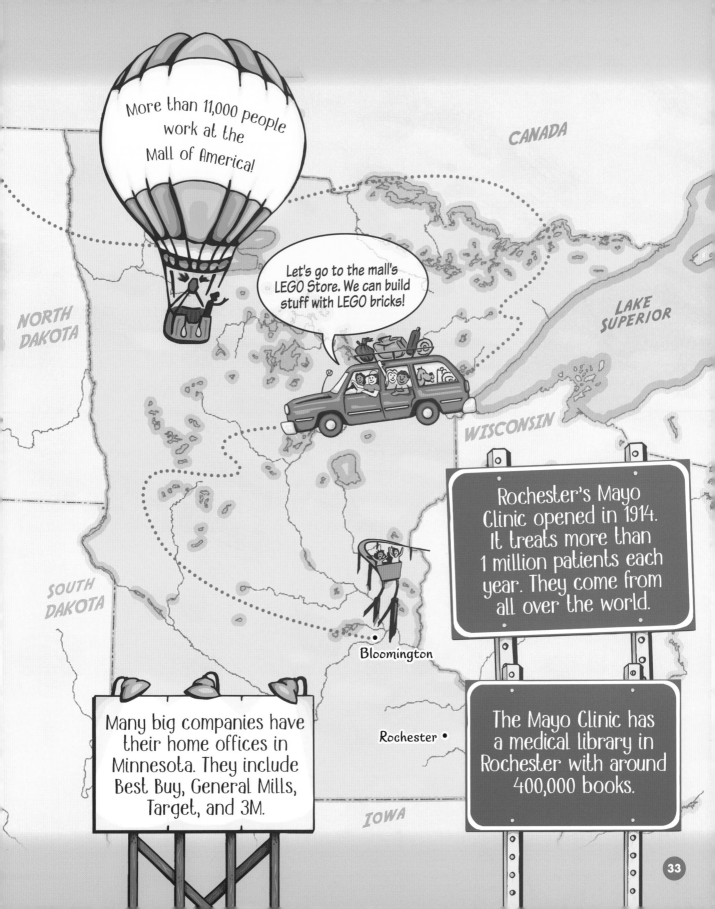

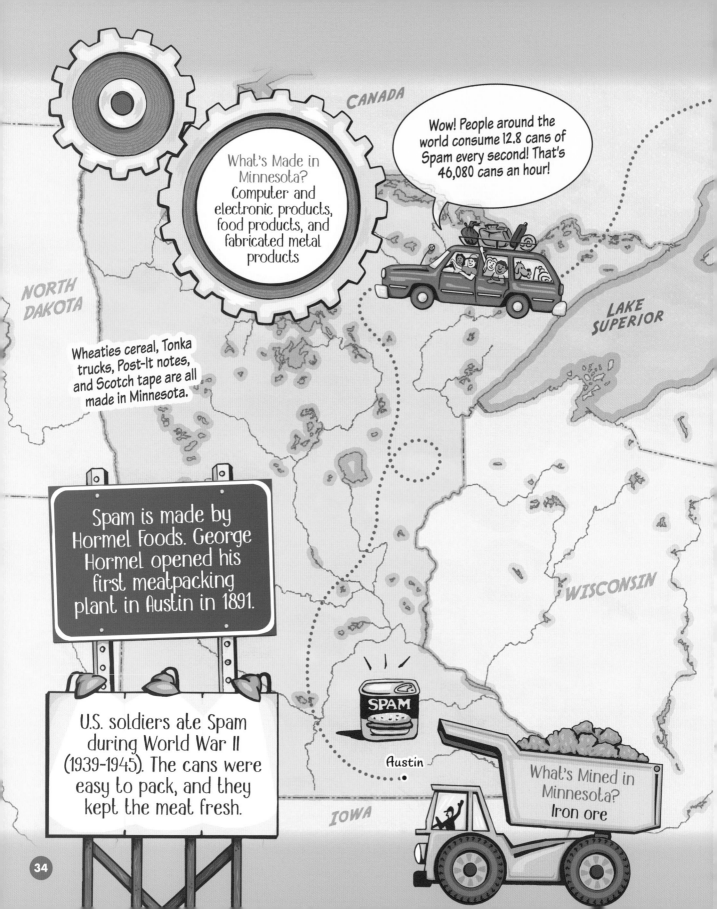

AUSTIN'S SPAM MUSEUM

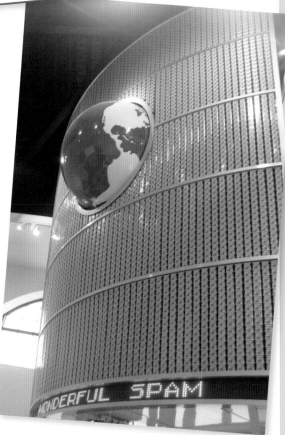

Do you like Spam? Not the computer kind. This Spam is a famous canned lunch meat. Just visit the Spam Museum!

First you see the towering Wall of Spam. It's made of thousands of Spam cans. Then you can watch videos about Spam. You can take the Spam Exam. Or try getting some Spam into a can!

Meat processing is a big industry in Minnesota. Cattle, hogs, turkeys, and chickens provide the meat. It goes to meat plants. There it's ground up and frozen. Finally, it's packaged for stores.

Minnesota factories make many other products. But only Spam has its own museum!

The Wall of Spam is made of Spam cans.

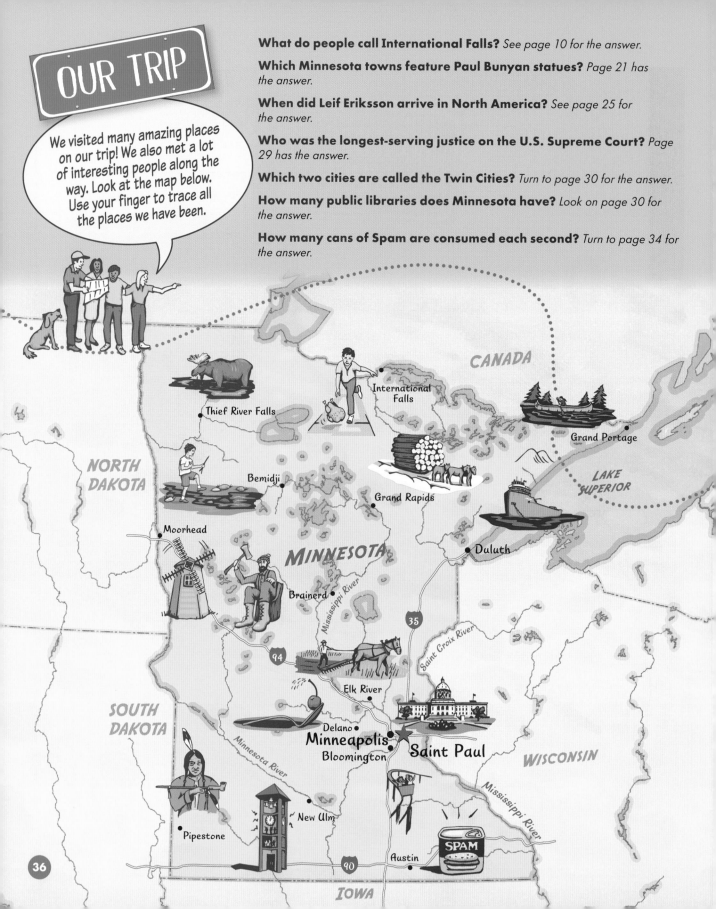

OUR TRIP

We visited many amazing places on our trip! We also met a lot of interesting people along the way. Look at the map below. Use your finger to trace all the places we have been.

What do people call International Falls? *See page 10 for the answer.*

Which Minnesota towns feature Paul Bunyan statues? *Page 21 has the answer.*

When did Leif Eriksson arrive in North America? *See page 25 for the answer.*

Who was the longest-serving justice on the U.S. Supreme Court? *Page 29 has the answer.*

Which two cities are called the Twin Cities? *Turn to page 30 for the answer.*

How many public libraries does Minnesota have? *Look on page 30 for the answer.*

How many cans of Spam are consumed each second? *Turn to page 34 for the answer.*

CANADA

Thief River Falls

International Falls

Grand Portage

LAKE SUPERIOR

NORTH DAKOTA

Bemidji

Grand Rapids

Moorhead

Duluth

MINNESOTA

Brainerd

Mississippi River

35

Saint Croix River

94

Elk River

SOUTH DAKOTA

Minnesota River

Delano

Minneapolis

Bloomington

Saint Paul

WISCONSIN

Mississippi River

Pipestone

New Ulm

SPAM

Austin

90

IOWA

State flag

State seal

STATE SYMBOLS

State bird: Common loon

State butterfly: Monarch butterfly

State drink: Milk

State fish: Walleye

State flower: Pink and white lady's slipper

State gemstone: Lake Superior agate

State grain: Wild rice

State muffin: Blueberry muffin

State mushroom: Morel

State tree: Red pine

STATE SONG

"HAIL! MINNESOTA"

Words by Truman E. Rickard and Arthur E. Upson, music by Truman E. Rickard

Minnesota, hail to thee!
Hail to thee, our state so dear!
Thy light shall ever be
A beacon bright and clear.
Thy sons and daughters true
Will proclaim thee near and far,
They shall guard thy fame
And adore thy name;
Thou shalt be their Northern Star.

Like the stream that bends to sea,
Like the pine that seeks the blue,
Minnesota, still for thee
Thy sons are strong and true.
From the woods and waters fair;
From the prairies waving far,
At thy call they throng
With their shout and song,
Hailing thee their Northern Star.

That was a great trip! We have traveled all over Minnesota! There are a few places we didn't have time for, though. Next time, we plan to visit Apple Jack Orchards in Delano. Visitors can pick raspberries and apples. In the fall, people can buy pumpkins!

FAMOUS PEOPLE

Chin, Leeann (1933–2010), restaurant owner

Coen, Ethan (1957–), **Joel** (1954–), filmmakers

DiCamillo, Kate (1964–), children's author

Dylan, Bob (1941–), musician and songwriter awarded the 2016 Nobel Prize in Literature

Fitzgerald, F. Scott (1896–1940), author

Fitzgerald, Larry (1983–), football player

Garland, Judy (1922–1969), actor and singer

Keillor, Garrison (1942–), radio host and writer

Lewis, Sinclair (1885–1951), novelist

Madden, John (1936–), football coach and broadcaster

Mauer, Joe (1983–), baseball player

Mayo, William Worrall (1819–1911), doctor who founded the Mayo Clinic

Mondale, Walter (1928–), politician

O'Brien, Tim (1946–), author

Pratt, Chris (1979–), actor

Prince (1958–2016), musician and songwriter

Ryder, Winona (1971–), actor

Schulz, Charles M. (1922–2000), creator of the comic strip Peanuts

Ventura, Jesse (1951–), wrestler and former governor of Minnesota

Vonn, Lindsey (1984–), Olympic skier

Wilkins, Roy (1901–1981), civil rights leader

WORDS TO KNOW

cargo (KAR-goh) goods that are transported in large amounts on some kind of vehicle

culture (KUHL-chur) a group of people's customs, beliefs, and way of life

horsepower (HORS-pow-ur) a unit that measures an engine's power

immigrants (IM-uh-gruhnts) people who leave their home country and move to another country

industry (IN-duh-stree) a type of business

lumberjacks (LUHM-bur-jaks) workers in the logging business who cut down trees and transport logs

ore (OR) rock that contains valuable metals such as iron or gold

rendezvous (RON-day-voo) French word for a meeting

reservation (rez-ur-VAY-shuhn) land set aside by the U.S. government for Native Americans

tall tales (TAHL TAILZ) stories that are exaggerated and hard to believe

traditions (truh-DISH-unz) long-held customs

voyageurs (voy-uh-ZHURZ) people working for fur companies who traveled between the wilderness and trading posts

TO LEARN MORE

IN THE LIBRARY
Dwyer, Helen, and Sierra Adare. *Ojibwe History and Culture.*
New York, NY: Gareth Stevens Publishing, 2012.

Howell, Brian. *Minnesota Vikings.* Mankato, MN: The Child's World, 2016.

ON THE WEB
Visit our Web site for links about Minnesota:
childsworld.com/links

*Note to Parents, Teachers, and Librarians: We routinely verify our Web links to make sure
they are safe and active sites. So encourage your readers to check them out!*

PLACES TO VISIT OR CONTACT
Explore Minnesota Tourism
exploreminnesota.com/index.aspx
121 7th Place E
Metro Square, Suite 100
Saint Paul, MN 55101
800/847-4866
For more information about traveling in Minnesota

Minnesota Historical Society
mnhs.org
345 West Kellogg Boulevard
Saint Paul, MN 55102
651/259-3000
For more information about the history of Minnesota

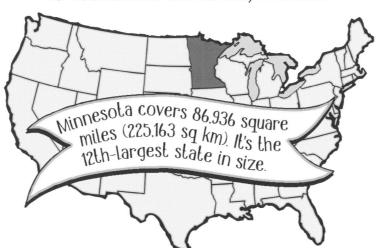

Minnesota covers 86,936 square miles (225,163 sq km). It's the 12th-largest state in size.

INDEX

Bye, North Star State.
We had a great time.
We'll come back soon!